The Wilds of Canada

JOHN CADIZ

DOUBLEDAY CANADA

FOR MY DAUGHTER, CATHERINE

CANADIAN CATALOGUING IN PUBLICATION DATA

Cadiz, John
        The Wilds of Canada

ISBN 0–385–25537–3

1. National characteristics, Canadian - Caricatures and cartoons. 2. Canada - Social life and customs - Caricatures and cartoons. 3. Canadian wit and humor, Pictorial. I. Title.

NC1449.C33A4 1995   741.5'971   C95–931222–8

Cover design by Heidy Lawrance Associates
Printed and bound in Canada

Published in Canada by
Doubleday Canada Limited
105 Bond Street
Toronto, Ontario
M5B 1Y3

I'd never given much thought to doing a book until my editor, Susan Folkins, approached me. I quickly learned that it entailed much more than randomly throwing together a bunch of drawings between two covers. She once joked — after I had missed yet another deadline — that I brought out the worst in her. I hope that through her gentle guidance she in turn has managed to bring out something better in me. Thank you, Susan.

OH CANADA!
OUR HOME ON NATIVE LAND
TRA LA LA LA
LA LA LA LA LA LA
TRA LA LA LA LA
LA LA LA LA LA
THE TRUE NORTH
STRONG AND FREE
LA LA LA LA LA
LA LA LA
CADIZ

INTRODUCTION

AS A CHILD GROWING UP IN TRINIDAD I was once shown a photograph of a relative in the middle of what appeared to be a mashed potato fight. Only later was it explained to me that the mashed potatoes were really snow and that this white stuff fell from the sky in a cold place called Canada.

One Christmas not long afterwards my parents gave me a weather kit. It was supposed to enable me to forecast snow, sleet, fog and other mysterious events. After labouring for weeks in anticipation of cold fronts and huge snowfalls, I finally realized that in Trinidad it was always either hot and sunny or hot and rainy. The only time the temperature dropped below 70 degrees was when I put the thermometer in the fridge and stuck my head inside to "breathe mist."

By the time I arrived in Canada I was wise enough to know that it wasn't *always* snowing and that it wasn't *always* winter. But I still wasn't quite prepared for kids on street corners with sticks and large nets yelling "CAR!" or total strangers immediately discussing the weather every time I stepped into an elevator.

What continues to surprise me most, however, is the number of people outside Canada who still believe this country is buried in snow. Only recently did I realize that this fiction is perpetuated by the Canadian government in order to keep defence spending down. After all, who would want to invade an iceberg? As a proud Canadian, I feel it is my duty to reveal the truth in the following pages. If you never hear from me again, well, you know what happened!

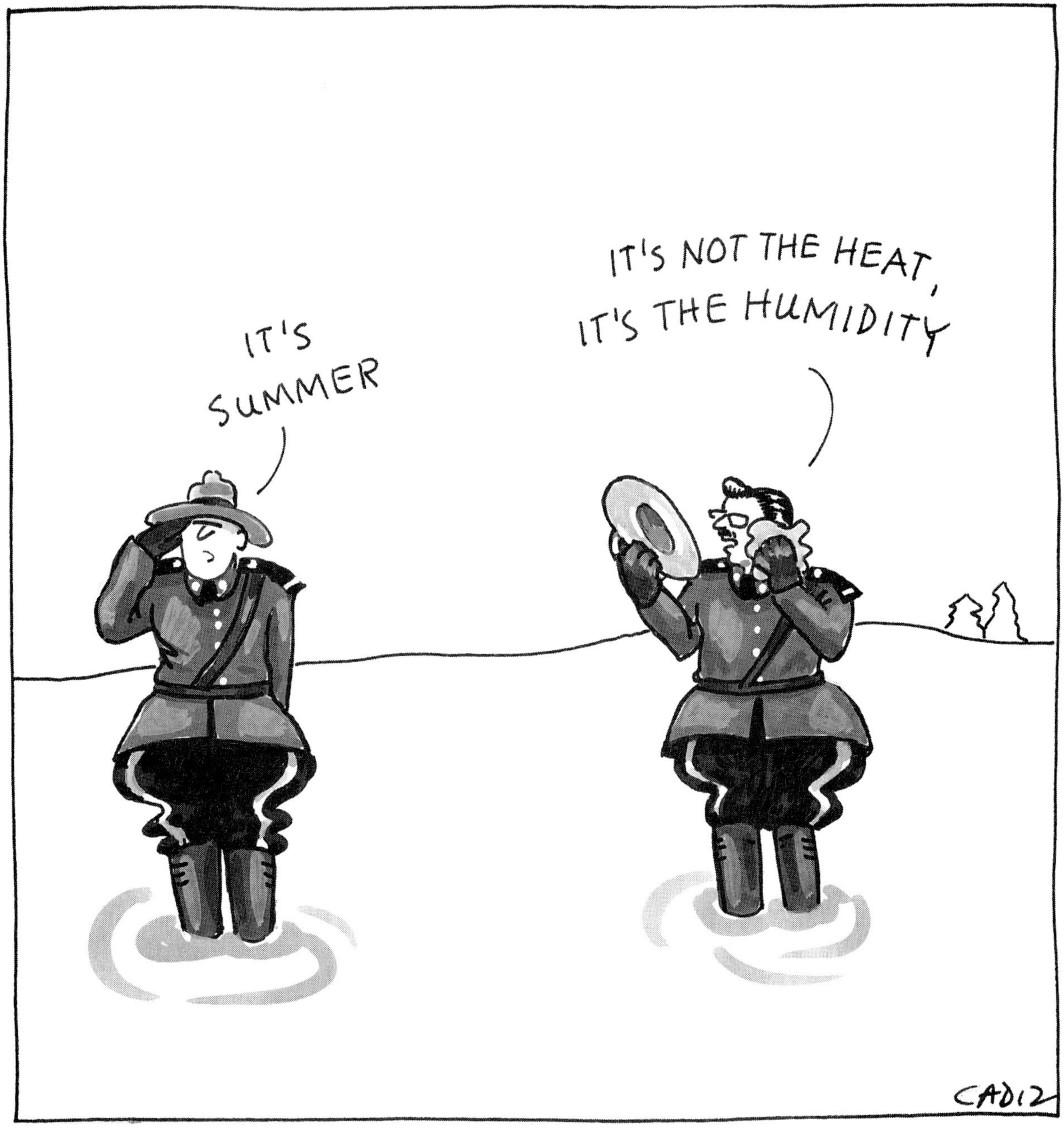
IT'S SUMMER
IT'S NOT THE HEAT, IT'S THE HUMIDITY
CADIZ

RUNNING OF THE BULLS

POLO BEARS CADIX

HOW BEAVERS GET THEIR TAILS

The Townhouses of Parliament

SPOT THE CANADIAN

CLASH OF THE MIGRANTS   CADIZ

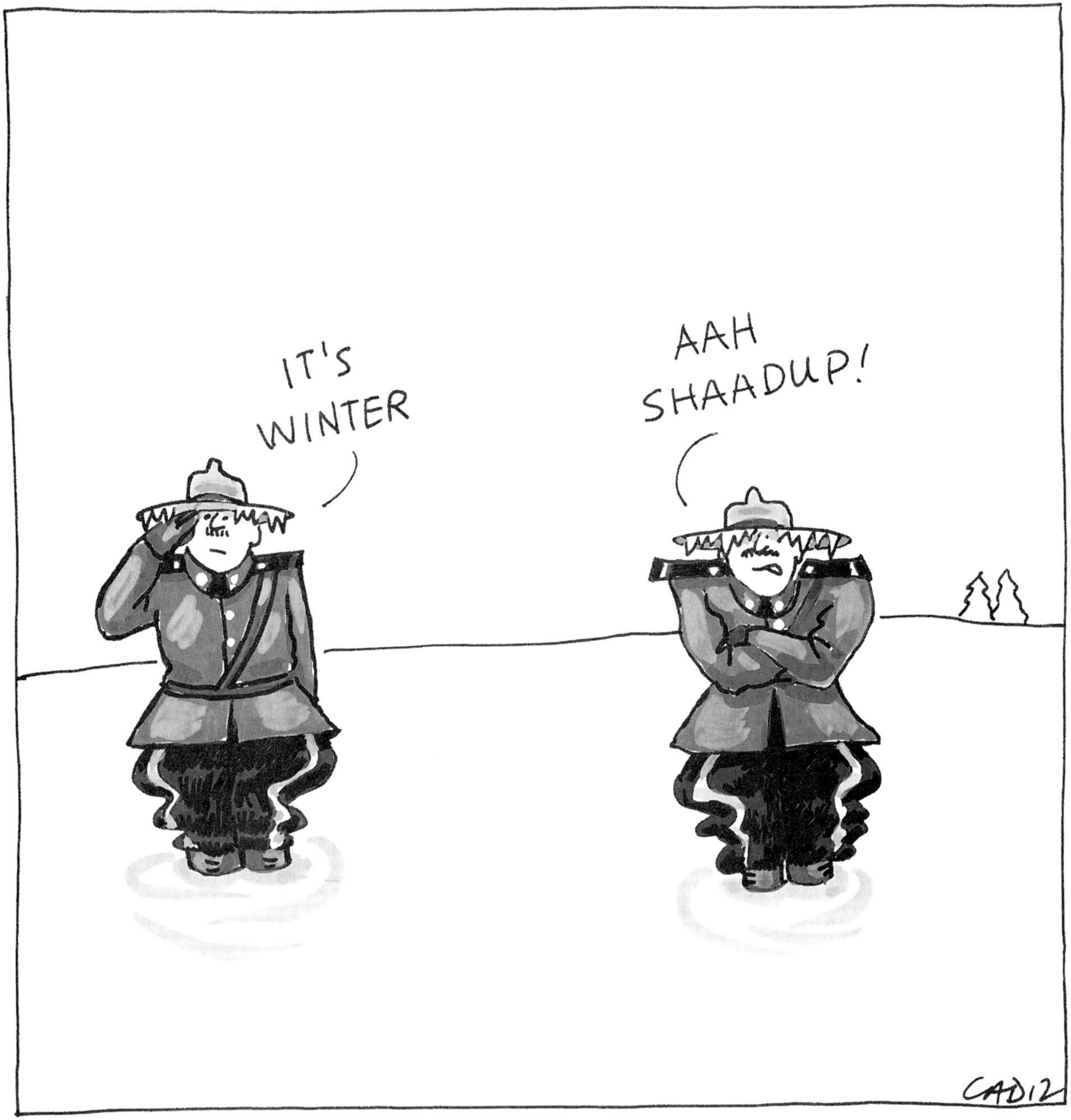
IT'S WINTER
AAH SHAADUP!
CAD12

PARLIAMENT TAKES A
RECESS ON THE RIDEAU

SNOWBIRDS   CADIZ

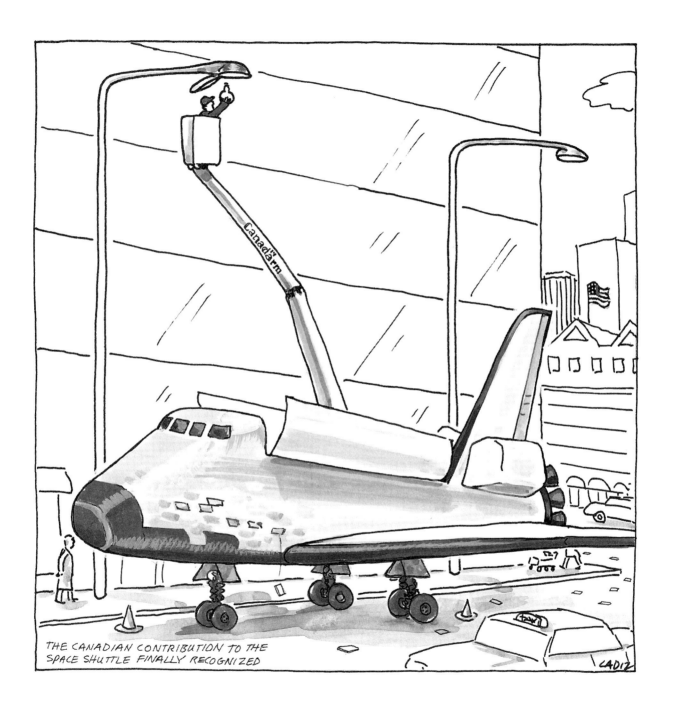

THE CANADIAN CONTRIBUTION TO THE
SPACE SHUTTLE FINALLY RECOGNIZED

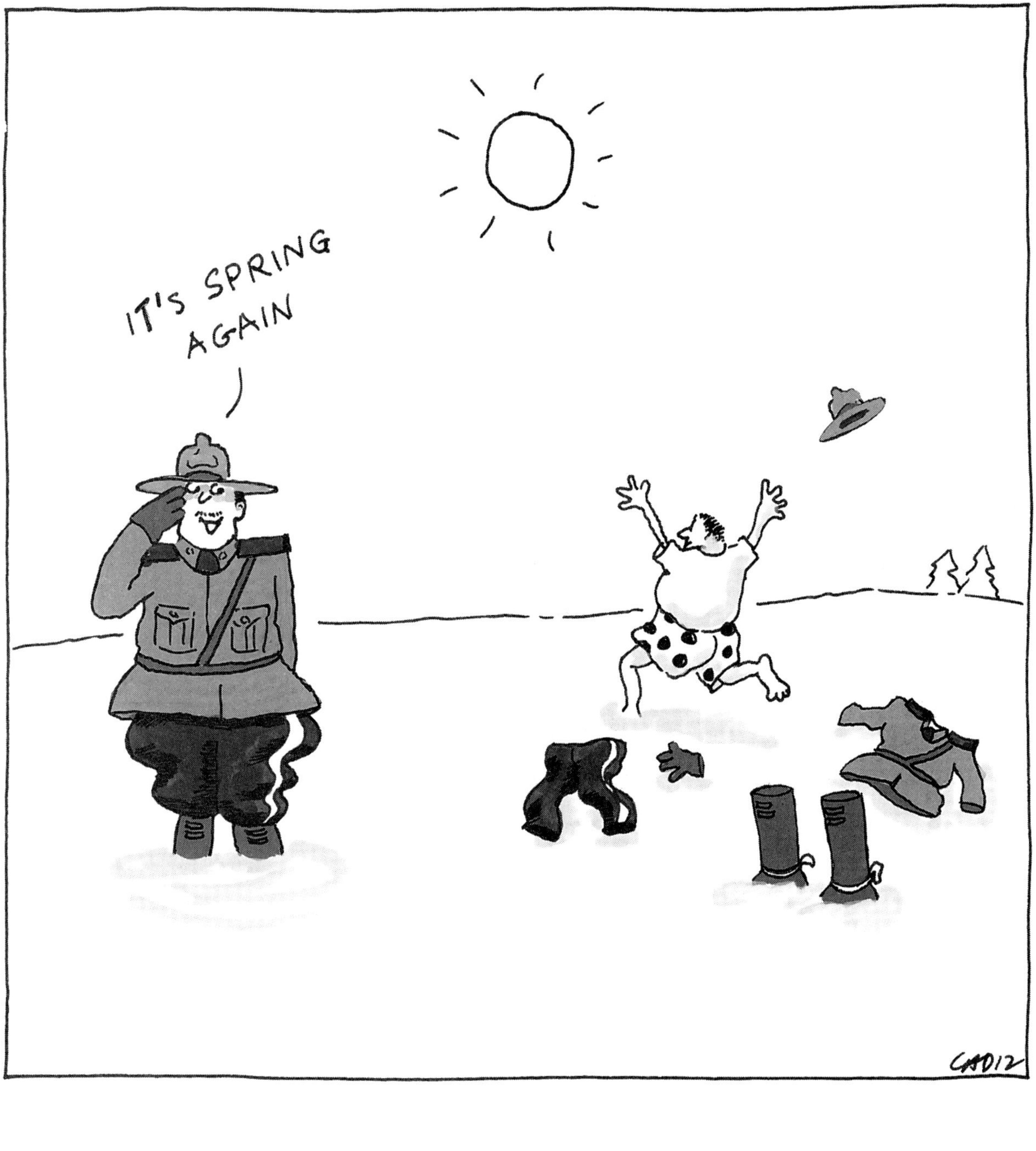
IT'S SPRING AGAIN
CADIZ

Select **Wilds of Canada**® images are available on T-shirts, sweatshirts, mugs, magnets, and greeting cards. For the name of a Wilds of Canada® dealer near you, please contact:

Scantrade International Ltd.
60 Horner Avenue
Toronto, Ontario
M8Z 4X3

Phone: (416) 259-1127
Fax: (416) 259-9303